AREA 51

The Truth Behind Roswell and the Area 51 Conspiracy

Phil Coleman

Table of Contents

Introduction

Just when did this place "happen"? When did people start to notice there was something there that was not there before?

Actually, August 1, 1955, when there was a high-speed test with the first U-2.

Area 51 has always been full of mystery and conspiracy theories.

It is a huge area of wasteland that was called for years simply: Area 51. To make it sound a little better, there was a period that it was called "Paradise Ranch," but who do they think they were fooling?

For years, it was not even allowed to be placed on a map of any kind.

There have been tons of theories and mystery shrouded in Area 51. There have been deathbed confessions regarding Area 51 that at one time were on YouTube but now they have been removed.

So, what do you say when a road to get there is named "Extraterrestrial Highway?"

The Whistleblowers of Area 51

Bob Lazar – he claimed that in 1989 he worked in Area 51, in the underground near the Papoose Lake inside the Papoose Range. He stated he had been contracted to work along-side alien spacecraft that the U.S. government had there in Area 51.

Bob was a physicist that worked in Area 51, so he was no dummy, and he had been sent there to work on reverse engineering of the aircraft's that had belonged to the aliens that had been captured and brought to the underground vault.

Bob had pictures of this little alien. If it is true, it makes one feel immensely sorry for this lifeform.

One thing that seems to stand clear among those who believe Lazar's stories. Much of the current technology we use is a result of reverse engineering from alien space craft; includes all kinds of technology like radios all the way to superconductors.

It is said that there is no way, that the human race as it is now could have possibly developed these technologies this fast without some alien model.

Many people disregard what Bob says as fiction are offended at the fact of what he claims, including a guy named Merlin, who has spent years and years speaking with Area 51 former employees who are angered about the fuss over E.T.

They say, "This is Earth technology, just good ole American ingenuity. Not any extraterrestrial stuff."

A 71-year-old mechanical engineer, Bill Uhouse, claimed he had been a former employee for Area 51 during the 50's. He claims that he worked on a "flying disc simulator" that had been on that crashed UFO and was being used to train U.S. Pilots. He also said that he worked with an alien named "J-Rod" and described him as a "telepathic translator."

Bill said J-Rod was Grey in color. Bill said that he worked with J-Rod so they could build a flight simulator to train the Air Force pilots to fly advanced USAF stealth air craft.

J-Rod himself had been the pilot of the UFO that had crashed.

Uhouse said that to talk to J-Rod, he used Grey alien technology that had been adapted to be used for humans. He was able to communicate with the Grey alien via telepathy that was assisted by very sophisticated translator software.

J-Rod taught humans how to fly the UFO.

Uhouse went on to say that there were different races within the Greys of the aliens.

They included Tall Greys, Short Greys, and then Greys with a size comparable to humans.

Uhouse died in 2009. It can no doubt be deduced going by deathbed confessions that extraterrestrial races and their civilizations are out there and they are technologically and scientifically far more advanced than we are.

It is the belief that during the administrations of Harry Truman and Dwight Eisenhower, is when construction began on the alien-government facilities. They were built for homes for the Grey, Reptilian, and Tall White Alien scientists.

SUPPOSEDLY, Eisenhower signed treaties with the extraterrestrial races.

The agreement signed with the Greys, Reptilians included that our government would let them perform bio-genetic research to design advanced forms of alien-human hybrids.

Our U.S. government allowed the aliens to get their hands on a limited number of humans to use as guinea pigs, for their bio-genetic research.

Conspiracy folks say Grey and Reptilian aliens needed to do this to save their races from extinction.

In return, the aliens give the U.S. access to alien technology, in particular, aerospace.

Now, there are rumors that Aliens are breaching their agreement and capturing more humans than they should. That sounds a little hard to believe - Almost conspiracy theories.

U.S. authorities cannot stop the violations. The facilities underground is armed with vast laboratories and special workshops. The underground areas have segments where the extraterrestrials live and captured humans are used as research guinea pigs are held as prisoners.

According to Ulhouse, to stick to their part of the bargain, there could be as many as hundreds or even thousands of the Grey aliens that are working with the PENTAGON!

Boyd Bushman, an ex-aerospace engineer also sent to Area 51 for a very long time has pictures of humanoid beings that do not belong to anything of this world. He confirms that staffs working in area 51 are a mixed lot of extraterrestrial beings and earthlings.

In 2004, there was a guy by the name of Dan Burisch (pseudonym of Dan Crain) said he worked on alien virus cloning at Area 51 beside an alien named "J-Rod." Burisch's credentials are much in question; however, as he was working as a parole officer in Las

Vegas in 1989 while he was also supposed to be earning a Ph.D. at New York State.

Existence of Area 51

They say that it is a facility of the U.S. Air Force and it is a remote part of Edwards Air Force Base that is highly classified. It is found in the Nevada Training and Test Range.

According to the CIA (Central Intelligence Agency, there are several names for this area, some of which are KXTA, Groom Lake, Homey Airport, Dreamland, Home Base, Paradise Ranch, and Watertown.

There is airspace around the field that is a Restricted Area 4808 North.

The main purpose for this base to the public is unknown; but based on past evidence; it supports developing and testing of weapons systems and experimental aircraft.

The intense secrecy that shrouds this place has caused it to be a frequent subject of UFO folklore and conspiracy theories.

The base itself has never been declared secret, but everything going on there is Top Secret and Sensitive.

July 2013 when the Freedom of Information Act requested information in 2005, the CIA for the first time acknowledged the bases existence.

Area 51 is in Nevada in the southern portion of the western U.S. and 83 miles northwest of Las Vegas. Smack in the middle and on the south shore of Groom Lake sits a large airfield of the military.

The U.S. Air Force acquired this land in 1955; they said to use for flight testing of aircraft, namely at the time the Lockheed U-2.

There was, in the beginning, a six by 10 mile base of sorts which is now called the "Groom Box." But now it measures 23 x 25 miles and is restricted airspace.

This area shares a border where the location of 739 and 928 nuclear tests were conducted by the United States Energy. The Yucca Mountain has a nuclear waste dump site 44 miles away from Groom Lake.

Groom Lake being a salt flat is used primarily, or so they say for runways for the Nellis Bombing Range Test Site airport.

The size of the lake is about 3.7 miles by 3 miles. This Lake is 25 miles south of the town Rachel, Nevada.

Where the name Area 51 came from is still unclear. The best guess is it comes from a grid numbering system by the Atomic Energy Commission. Area 51 is not part of the system, but it lies next to Area 15. No one knows.

In 1864 lead and silver were found in the south part of Groom Range. In the 1870's, Groome Lead Mines financed the mines giving it the name. Mining continued until

1918 and resumed after WWII until the early 1950's.

When WWII came along, the airstrip on Groom Lake started beginning service. They called it Indian Springs Air Force Auxiliary Field. It had two dirt runways that were 5000 feet long.

The test facility at Groom Lake for the U-2 program was established in 1955 by the CIA (Central Intelligence Agency) for developing the Lockheed U-2 Strategic Aircraft.

The director at the time, Richard Bissell, Jr., was told that due to the extreme secrecy of the project, the pilot training programs and the flight testing would not be done at Edwards Air Base or Palmdale.

An inspection team went out to Groom Lake. When they flew over it, they supposedly knew within thirty seconds that it was the perfect place.

The lakebed was a perfect landing strip for which they could do their testing of aircraft, and the mountain ranges would protect them from prying eyes. The CIA had the AEC acquire the land and designate it "Area 51" on the map.

Johnson himself called it "Paradise Ranch" so that the workers would be more encouraged to move to somewhere in the middle of nowhere. Most of the men just called it "the Ranch." Some of them called themselves Ranch hands.

Initially, it had a few shelters, some workshops, and trailer homes. At the end of three months, it had one paved runway, a control tower, three hangers, and essential accommodations for testing staff.

The only amenities were a volleyball court and a movie theater. There was a mess hall, fuel storage tanks, and several water wells.

July 1955, CIA, Lockheed staff, and Air Force started arriving. July 24th, they received its first U-2 delivery on a cargo plane.

Lockheed technicians came on a Douglas DC-3. To keep things secret, staff flew into Nevada on Monday mornings and went back to California Friday evenings.

In August 1959, Project OXCART was established. It was for antiradar studies, engineering designs, aerodynamic, structural tests and later on work on the Lockheed A-12.

October 1960 saw the beginning of a four-year construction project for Area 51. It was a double shift that worked.

The CIA received eight USAF F-101 Voodoos, two T-33 Shooting Star trainers, one C-130 Hercules for transporting cargo, U-3A for administrative use, a helicopter to be used for search and rescue, Cessna 180 to be used for liaison use, and an F-104 Starfighter to use as a chase plane.

February 26, 1962, the first A-12 test aircraft was trucked in from Burbank, reassembled and made its first flight April 26th. By then there was 1,000 staff members.

At first, anyone not connected with the testing be done at the time would be taken into the mess hall. They quickly stopped this because it was disrupting work and was just impractical.

The Area also saw the first Lockheed D-21 drone test on December 22, 1964. In January 1967, it was decided to phase out the CIA A-12 program.

After losing Gary Powers' U-2 over the Soviet Union, there began several discussions about using the A-12 OXCART like a drone. The Air Force finally agreed in October 1962 to the study of a high altitude, high speed, and drone aircraft. It would be called D-21.

The first launch of D-21 was on March 5, 1966, and it was successful. It flew 120 miles due to a limited amount of fuel.

The second flight was successful in April 1966, and the drone flew 1,200 miles, reaching 90,000 feet and Mach 3.3.

July 30, 1966, D-21 trial suffered from a non-start of the drone itself after separation and caused it to collide with the launch aircraft. The two crewmembers ejected and landed 150 miles off shore in the ocean. One was picked up by a helicopter; the other survived the breakup and the ejection, but drowned when water from the ocean filled his pressure suit.

Kelly Johnson said that was enough and canceled the entire program. There had been several D-21s already made, and instead of dumping all of them, Johnson proposed to the Air Force that they might launch them from a B-52H bomber.

Later than summer of 1967, modifying the D-21 (now called the D-21B) and the B-52Hs were done. They could restart the testing program. Test missions took off from Groom Lake and launches were over the Pacific.

The first test was on September 28, 1967, and it ended up in complete failure. There were several more flights, including two over China, one in 1969 and one in 1970. July 1971, Kelly Johnson got a wire that said cancel the whole D-21B program. The drones that were left went to dead storage.

In 1993, the D-21B's were released to museums.

During the Cold War, the United States tested and evaluated Soviet fighter aircraft that had been captured. Area 51 was supposed to have been where they were taken. As a matter of fact, they were supposed to have quite a collection of Soviet aircraft.

In August 1966, an Iraqi fighter pilot
defected and flew his MiG-21 on to Israel.
He had been ordered to drop napalm on
Iraqi Kurd villages. His aircraft was brought
to Groom Lake within a month's timeframe.

In 1968, they gained two MiG-17s that were
transferred from Israel because two Syrian
air force lieutenants got lost.

In early 1982, they were testing YF-117A
airplanes.

There are other aspects of activities of Area
51 that involved tests of 'acquired' Soviet-
radar systems gotten covertly. In November
of 1970, there was a project that was called
HAVE GLIB. Once account of this project
was that they used 'actual Soviet replicas

and systems set up as a complex' around Slater Lake.

The USAF gave these places name such as Kay, Mary, Kathy and Susan and arranged everything so it would be just like a Soviet air defense complex.

Now, when they declassified the F-117 program, the Air Force decided to bring in two other air programs into Area 51. Neither of these projects ever led to a production of an operational fleet however. Both have been declassified. There are some pictures and some fact sheets giving some details about the two secret programs which never really got off the ground.

There was one plane that was developed by the Northrop group along with the USAF and DARPA. It was TACIT BLUE, a battlefield plane to be used for surveillance and it was also known as the "Whale."

They started working on it in 1978 and got to finally fly it at Area 51 February 1982. The program for this air craft stopped in 1985 and it had flown a total of 135 times.

The fact sheet on this project showed that the goal was to 'demonstrate that with curved surfaces would make a difference in low radar return signal' and that TACIT BLUE could go to the front line of the battlefield without any fear of being seen on the enemy radar.

Then there was another plane that Area 51 worked on with McDonald Douglas (bought out in 1996 by Boeing) called the "Phantom Works" and some called it the Bird of Prey," after all it did resemble the Klingon from Star Trek.

But, it was declassified in 2002 because its techniques basically were already becoming obsolete.

Interestingly, there were two other projects that were connected to Area 51. One of them was used in a raid on May 2, 2001 and it was the raid that took down and killed Osama Ben Laden.

It was the stealth helicopter that took our Navy Seals up to the Abbottabad compound where Ben Laden was hiding. The other piece was a RQ-170 stealth drone that had been used to monitor what was going on in and around the compound.

The RQ-170 is an unmanned drone and it is intended to be used to provide surveillance and reconnaissance for our soldiers. This drone alone can save numerous lives and get in and out and send back invaluable information to our men.

Safety of our soldiers should be the first thing that is thought about for them, their families and for our country.

Commuters to Area 51 get there by travel on an unmarked Boeing 737 or 727. The planes leave from McCarran Airport in Las Vegas.

EG&G, the defense contractor, owns this terminal. Each plane uses the same name, "Janet" followed by three digits for calling into the control tower.

Airspace above Area 51 is called R-4808 and is totally restricted to any and all commercial and military flights not coming from the base itself.

Area 51 is classified as a (MOA) Military Operating Area. The borders have no fence, but orange poles mark the perimeter and warning signs are posted. The signs warn that photography isn't allowed and trespassing will result in a fine.

There are other signs that are more sobering: "Security is authorized to use deadly force on people who insist on trespassing."

Of course, the conspiracy folks wonder how many have died because they got caught tromping around on the grounds of Area 51. Most believe, however, that the trespassers are not dealt with so harshly.

Men in pairs that do not appear military are patrolling the perimeter. The guards are probably civilians hired from contract companies.

Most people call them "camo dudes," just because they wear desert storm camo. Camo dudes usually are seen driving around in a four-wheel-drive vehicle of some sort.

It seems that camo dudes have instructions to avoid the intruders and only act as deterrents. If someone appears to be an intruder, camo dudes will put a call into the sheriff, and he will deal with them.

There have been times when camo dudes have confronted trespassers, taking their film or any recording devices and trying to scare the trespassers. Sometimes, a helicopter will fly over or hover around to harass or scare.

With all the sensors planted everywhere around the base, no one can get past them. They are supposed to detect movement, but there are those who think they can tell the difference between human and animal.

Since Area 51 is a wildlife area, it would seem to be important that a warning device could not be tripped by animals.

Some feel that they are ammonia sensors being able to tell between human ammonia and animal ammonia.

One Rachel resident, Chuck Clark got his hand on several sensors from around the perimeter. He was found out and ordered to put them back or face some serious fines. Reportedly, he complied.

Everyone is interested in what is going on in Area 51 today. Here are a few ideas, not saying they are in stone, but very real possibilities:

- A transport aircraft to move troops out and in areas of conflict without ever being detected. Many saw this as a critical need.

- Stealth helicopter. Some say that these already exist and are in use, but have never been revealed to the public.

- There is a need for a stealth airplane so it can neutralize ground targets.

- Other research projects that are rumored are proton beams, anti-gravity devices, and cloaking technology.

The A-12 plane is a very impressive handsome aircraft that was developed in

Area 51. It flies at speeds higher than 2,200 mph and must have 186 miles to turn around.

Many people still do not believe that man landed on the moon or ever set foot there and that it was staged out in Area 51. They also say that the astronauts tested life support systems and lunar rovers at the atomic testing grounds just next door.

Legal Status of Area 51

October 22, 2015, a judge signed papers taking land that had belonged to a Nevada family since the 1870s and turned it over to the USAF so they could expand Area 51.

This family had owned the property since Abraham Lincoln was president.

The Sheahan Family had owned the old mine and knew they had a terrible battle going up against the U.S. government. They knew ahead of time that it would probably be taken from them through eminent domain.

The government condemned the property one month after the family declined their offer of a $5.2 million buyout. They knew their land was worth a lot more than that because of all the mineral rights for it and the number of acres it contained.

The land has a lot of ore in it and on the land, there is mining equipment, buildings and the remains of loved ones buried who worked the mines since 1870.

The family has also had to suffer from radiation drifting from nuclear shots during the 1950s and the 1960s.

The family feels like it has been a 60-year Black Ops, AEC, CIA and you could go on forever said Joe Sheahan, the heir.

Since the air force has condemned the property, the value of the land is now only $1.5 million.

The judge said that the land that was being taken was to address safety and security connected with testing and training.

How wrong can this be?

The government's amount of information that they are willing to tell is at best very little. The area around the Lake is off-limits permanently to all civilians and even to regular air traffic of the military. Security checks are constant; no weapons or cameras of any kind are allowed.

1994 saw litigation from five unnamed contractors that were civilians and the widows of two contractors, Robert Frost and Walter Kasza against the USAF and the US EPA (Environmental Protection Agency).

They were represented by Jonathan Turley, a law professor at George Washington University. Their allegations were that they had been exposed to large amounts of unknown chemicals that were burned in trenches and open pits at Area 51.

Biopsies taken from these individuals were analyzed, and in the biopsies, there were found high levels of dibenzofuran, trichloroethylene, and dioxin. They also alleged that they had suffered skin, respiratory and liver injuries due to their working at Area 51; and that this fact had caused the mortality of Frost and Kasza.

The suit asked for compensation for their injuries, due to the claim that the USAF had not handled the toxic materials properly, and that the EPA had failed to enforce the Resource Conservation and Recovery Act (the act that governs the handling of dangerous materials).

The families also wanted detailed reports about the chemicals to which they had been exposed, in hopes that those still living might be better served medically.

Congressman Lee Hamilton, a former chair of the House Intelligence Committee, told Lesley Stahl on 60 minutes, "The USAF is classifying all this information to protect Area 51 from a lawsuit."

And the government wonders why the public does not trust them?

The President still raises the issue every year trying to determine the Groom exception. This, raised by the President and other very specific wording used in other communications by the government, is the only real recognition the U.S. Government has given that Groom Lake is more than a part of the Nellis complex.

There was an unclassified memo that went out on safe handling of Nighthawk F-117 material that got posted on an Air Force web site apparently inadvertently in 2005.

This material was what had been discussed by the complainants in the lawsuit. The information the government had declared was classified. The memo was gone quickly after journalists were made aware of it.

In 2007 in December, it was noticed by pilots that the base was now appearing on their navigation systems latest Jeppesen revision. The airport code being KXTA and was listed as "Homey Airport."

This inadvertently published information of airport data was soon followed by an announcement that student pilots needed to be warned about KXTA, and they were not to ever consider it a destination or waypoint.

There is signage all around the base perimeter that advises deadly force will be used against all trespassers.

Early most mornings, some eagle-eyed visitors can spot lights in the sky moving around and up and down. It is not a UFO. In reality, it is the semi-secret commuter airline contracted that they call "Janet" that transports employees in from Las Vegas to Area 51.

Fiction or fact, the alien theme is a huge tourism draw. In 1996, Nevada renamed Route 375, "Extraterrestrial Highway" and gave destinations like the Alien Research Center and an Alien Cathouse which is supposedly the only alien-themed brothel in the entire world.

If you are planning on walking to Area 51, plan carefully. It is a desert. Bring snacks, bring the right clothing for the cold nights and the horrible hot days and bring LOTS of water.

Your phone will probably not work nor you're GPS. Have real maps. It will be hard to find gas stations, so have spare tires and extra fuel.

Whatever you do, DO NOT trespass. Arrests and heavy fines await you for this infraction.

UFO & Other Conspiracy Theories

Along with its secretive reputation and the connection to aircraft research, along with odd reports of unusual phenomena, has caused Area 51 to focus on modern UFO and the conspiracy theories surrounding them.

June 24, 1947, Kenneth Arnold reported that while he was piloting his private plane, he saw something that was flying in the sky like a saucer would if you skipped it across the water. Thus, the name of the "flying saucer" was born.

Some of the activities causing all of this include:

- The examination, reverse engineering, and storage of crashed spacecraft with aliens (including items that were supposed to be recovered from the UFO crash site at Roswell), the study of occupants (dead and living), aircraft manufacture based on technology used by aliens.

- Joint undertakings or meetings with extraterrestrials.

- Developing of exotic weapons of energy for Strategic Defense Initiative or other programs for weapons.

- Developing means to control the weather

- Developing time travel and technology for teleportation.

- Developing of exotic and unusual propulsion systems that are related to the Aurora Program.

- Activities aligned with one world government (Illuminati) or Majestic 12 organization.

Many theories involve concern the underground areas at Groom or Papoose Lake. They claim transcontinental railroad underground system and alien based engineering technology.

During the mid-1950's, civilian aircraft would fly under 20,000 feet while

Military would fly under 40,000 feet. When the U-2 started flying, it went above 60,000 feet, and one of the side effects it caused was an increased sighting of UFOs.

They were usually seen during the early evening. When pilots were flying west and saw U-2's silver wings reflecting the setting sun, it would give the aircraft its own "fiery" appearance.

Many of the UFO sightings came to USAF Project Blue Book, which is where UFO sightings were investigated, by air-traffic controllers and by letters sent to the government.

Most of the UFO sightings could be dismissed, but they could not reveal to the people who wrote the letters the actual truth about what they did see.

Veterans working in Area 51 will admit that their work while there in that time frame more than likely prompted many of the UFO sightings.

The shape of OXCART had a wide, disk-like fuselage so it could carry large amounts of fuel. Commercial pilots flying over Nevada at around dusk could look up and see the bottom of an OXCART flying overhead at 2,000 plus miles per hour and with the suns reflection it would make anyone think UFO.

They felt the rumors helped keep Area 51 in secrecy. And, so it did.

In June 2015, the head of NASA did confirm that aliens did in fact exist, but they were not hidden at Area 51.

We know today, which thousands, if not millions of other planets, many probably very much similar to our 'earth' exist. So, it seems fair to say that we will find out that life or evidence of life elsewhere will be found.

People living in towns nearby report sightings of strange lights that appear as if are hovering over Area 51. Per eye witnesses, the lights do not look like lights on fighter jets or any other earthly aviation type units.

Supposedly there is an autopsy video (http://proofofalien.com/the-truth-of-roswell-alien-autopsy-video/) of the alien that was taped during the autopsy held inside Area 51. This is said to be evidence that Area 51 has a strong connection with the little guys.

The corpse of this particular alien is thought to have been from the Roswell site in New Mexico.

When you go this website, you will find that this documentary was found to be a hoax, as real as it looked. Ray Santillilli, declared that he received $100,000 and got his film from an 82-year-old American who was a retired photographer.

You will notice that this video is no longer available for viewing, but the corpse on the website sure looks real if you are into looking at dead aliens.

July 1947, the time of the alleged Roswell, New Mexico alien crash was what really put Area 51 on the map.

It was the first week of July 1947, and a UFO crashed on the ranch of W.W. "Mack" Brazel in Roswell, New Mexico.

Later, Brazel found some debris from close to the crash site, so he and wife, Loretta and Floyd Proctor's son got on their horses and rode out to check on their sheep since there had been a bad thunderstorm the evening before.

As they were riding out to where the sheep were, Brazel noticed odd pieces of what looked like some metal scattered here and there over a pretty large area.

When he looked closer, he noticed something that looked like a shallow trench that was several hundred feet in length and it had been gouged down into the ground.

Brazel said what was so odd was the metal. He had never seen any metal like that before. They gathered some of it up and took the large pieces to his shed and a piece or two over to show the Proctors.

Mrs. Proctor remembers when he came to the house with the strange looking metal.

The Proctors told him it might be something from one of the UFOs everyone had been seeing and he needs to tell the Chaves County Sheriff, George Wilcox.

So, a couple of days later, Brazel went into Roswell and reported the weird incident to the Sheriff. He, in turn, reported it to Major Marcel who served as an intelligence officer and was stationed at Roswell Army Air Field.

History of UFO crashes was kept in a book that UFO researchers, Kevin Randle and Don Schmitt say that they kept their research recorded in and it did show that military radar was tracking some flying object they could not identify over southern New Mexico for about four days. They noticed on July 4th, 1947, that the object had looked like it went down about 30-40 miles from Roswell.

The book records that eyewitness Bill Woody, who lived near Roswell to the east, said he remembered being outside that night when he saw a brilliant light plunge to the earth.

Well, the debris site was then closed to everyone for several days so the wreckage could be cleaned up. Randle and Schmitt said that when Woody and his dad tried to find the area where the crash had happened, that they were stopped by military staff and were told to get out of the area.

Randle and Schmitt said after they had received orders, they were sent to investigate Brazel's report. They followed the rancher to where he lived. They spent the night at his place, and Marcel looked over a large piece of metal that Brazel had brought in from out in the pasture.

Monday morning, July 7th, Marcel got to take his first steps out onto the debris field. Marcel could determine which direction it had come from, and which way it had been going.

Marcel said the debris was everywhere covering a large area. He guessed about ¾ of a mile long and about a few hundred feet in width. In the debris field, there were little bits of metal. Marcel finally took out his cigarette lighter out to see if it would burn.

Not only did they find metal, but they found weightless "I" beam like pieces that measured three-eighths inch by one-quarter inch with none of them being very long. You could not get it to bend or break.

He also described metal no thicker than tinfoil that you could not destruct no matter what you did to it.

Marcel filled his car up and thought he would stop by his house on the way back to the base to let his family see this unusual stuff. He had just never seen anything like this before!

May 1990, Jesse Marcel Jr. was hypnotized so they could find out how much he knew. He said he could remember his dad waking him up during the night, and then he went out to the car with his dad and helped him carry in a large box that was full of this debris. Once they got it in the house, they dumped it all on the kitchen floor.

Meanwhile, a young mortician by the name of Glenn Dennis was working for the Ballard Funeral Home and had received some very unusual calls one afternoon that came from the RAAF.

The bases mortuary officer needed to get his hands on some small specially sealed coffins and wanted to know how to preserve bodies that had been exposed to the weather for a few days and avoid contamination of the tissue.

Dennis said that later that evening, he drove over to the base hospital, where he noticed large pieces of wreckage that had weird engravings on some of the pieces sticking out of the back of the ambulance.

He had gone on into the hospital and was visiting with a nurse he knew when all of a sudden he was threatened and forced to leave by military police.

July 8, 1947, Walter Haut, the RAAF public info officer, had finished up a press release he had been ordered to write. It stated that wreckage from crashed dish was removed.

He then gave out copies to two radio stations and two local newspapers. But by 2:26, the story could be found on the Associated Press.

It simply stated that USAF was here today and it stated that the flying disc had been located.

Calls began coming into the base from every corner of the world. Lt. Shirkey watched as Military Police moved wreckage onto a C-54 from a Transport Unit.

So, he could see better, Shirkey moved around Col. Blanchard, who was not happy with all the calls that were coming in. Blanchard decided to leave the debris field and left instructions for everyone that he was 'on leave.'

Headquarters Gets Involved

Blanchard had sent Marcel to work at another Air field and report to the Brig.

Marcel revealed to Haut years later that he had taken some of the debris into Ramey's office so Ramey could see what they had found. The material was left lying there so when Ramey came back he could see it, it would be there for him to look at and go over.

When Ramey got back, he wanted to see the exact location where the debris had been found. So, Ramey and Marcel went down the hall to a map room. When they got back to the room, all the original wreckage was "gone," and a weather balloon had been spread out all over the floor. Major Cashon took a picture of Marcel with the weather balloon.

At this point, it was reported that Ramey realized that it was parts of a weather balloon. He was told by General Dubose that this was going to be a "cover story." The balloon part that is what would be told to the public.

Later on, that day, in the afternoon, the original press release about the UFO was rescinded, and all copies picked up from the newspaper offices and the radio stations.

The next day, July 9th, another press release went out stating that the 509th Bomb Group had mistakenly identified a weather balloon for a UFO.

Then on July 9th, when the reports went out that the crashed object was a weather balloon, there were cleanup crews out there getting rid of the evidence.

Bud Payne, another rancher at Corona, was out trying to round up a stray cow when the military saw him and he was physically carried off the ranch owned by the Fosters. Broadcasters Walt Whitmore and Judd Roberts were told to go away when they approached the debris area.

So, let me see, Government ground belongs to the government and Our land that we paid for, not land the government paid for, belongs to the government as well. Is that what it sounds like to you?

When the wreckage "FROM THE UFO" was brought in to the Area 51, it got crated and stored in a hangar.

Now, meanwhile, back in town, Lyman Strickland and Walt Whitmore ran into their buddy, Mack Brazel, that was being escorted to Roswell Paper Office by not one, not two, but THREE military officers.

Brazel totally ignored Strickland and Whitmore, which was totally unlike Brazel. When he got to the newspaper office, his story had changed.

He told the newspaper now that he found all the debris on June 14. He also told them that he had found weather devices two other times, but what he found this time was not a weather balloon.

The Associated Press story carried this: "Reports of flying saucers whizzing through the sky fell off sharply today as the Army and the Navy began a concentrated campaign to stop the rumors."

The story went on to report that the AAF Headquarters located in Washington had "given blistering rebuke to the Roswell officers."

From that time, the military has worked hard at trying to convince the news that what was found at Roswell was just a weather balloon.

Dennis met with the nurse the very next day. She let him know that bodies were found in that wrecked UFO and she drew pictures of them on a prescription pad. In a few days, that nurse was transferred to England; her whereabouts to this day remain unknown.

At the time, a farmer/rancher; Mac Brazel found some strange looking metal strewn over his farm. He picked it up and took it the authorities in Roswell. Commanding Officer, Colonel Blanchard ordered an investigation. A statement was issued to the press that said they had found some "flying disk."

After this, the Army came back and retracted what they had said earlier and said it was probably shrapnel that was from a weather balloon. It took 30 years for Roswell conspiracy theories to really get started growing from this one incident.

95% of Americans have heard or read something about UFOs. 57% believe they are real.

Former Presidents Reagan and Carter claim that they have seen a UFO. Many are convinced that the U.S. government but mainly the CIA are the ones involved in a massive cover-up and conspiracy of the whole issue.

October 20, 1960, Minneapolis, Minnesota- The CIA becomes concerned about the Soviets and UFO reports. They checked the Soviet press for any UFO sightings, but could not find any.

They felt that with the absence of reports, this could only mean one thing and that was deliberate Soviet Government involvement. They felt that the USSR's use of UFO's was for psychological warfare.

They worried that the United States warning system of the air ways might be deliberately overloaded due to UFO sightings, giving the Soviets and edge to surprise the US with a nuclear attack.

The tense Cold War situation and the capabilities of the Soviets made the CIA nervous, and they saw serious national security issues involving flying saucers.

The CIA felt that the Soviets could and might use UFO sighting reports to cause mass panic and hysteria in the United States.

The CIA also felt that the Soviets might try to use UFO sightings and overload US early air warning systems so we would not be able to determine phantom from real targets.

Marshall Chadwell, then Assistant Director of OSI, felt the problem was so important that the National Security Council needed to know about all of this so that a coordinated effort could be made.

Chadwell explained the situation to DCI Smith in December 1952. He wanted action because he was convinced that there was something going on that needed immediate action.

On December 4, 1952, the (IAC) Intelligence Advisory Committee took up the concerns about the UFOs. The idea about the UFOs was informally discussed.

The committee decided the DCI should review this. Major General John Samford, Air Force Intelligence Director, said they had his full cooperation.

At this time Chadwell notices that the British were looking into UFO phenomena. The Brits had noted during an air show recently that a Royal Air Force pilot and some Senior Military Officials had seen a "perfect flying saucer."

In 1953, the Robertson Panel was assembled. They were all nonmilitary scientists that were to study UFO issues.

They found that there was nothing there that indicated any direct threat to national security and no evidence of extraterrestrials.

After the Robertson report was given, officials put UFO issues on a back burner.

To US military and political leaders, the Soviet Union was a dangerous opponent by the mid-1950s. The Soviet's, were leading in the progression in guided missiles, and nuclear weapons and it was very alarming. During the summer of 1949, the USSR had detonated an atomic bomb.

August 1953, just nine months after the U.S. tested a hydrogen bomb, along came the Soviets and detonated one.

Concern about the danger of the Soviets going to attack the U.S. continued to grow, and UFO sightings made U.S. policymakers more uneasy.

There were more reports of UFOs over Afghanistan, and Europe prompted more concern that Soviets were way ahead in this area. CIA already knew that Canadians and British were experimenting with "flying saucers."

People had started doubting the urban legend about a flying saucer landing in the desert.

But then came a remarkable revelation by an Air Force pilot named French who told that there were two UFO crashes at Roswell and most people do not know that.

The first UFO had been shot down by a U.S. plane that had been taking off from

White Sands, N.M. It had been shot with a weapon that was electronic pulse-type and disabled all the controls of the UFO, causing it to crash.

French, in 1947, was being checked out in an altitude chamber, which was required annually for officers, was extremely specific in the way the military brought the UFO down which he was sure was here from another world.

French said when they smacked it with that electromagnetic pulse – bam- out went their electronics, and they couldn't even control the UFO.

French was someone you could believe, and he had held multiple positions in

Military Intelligence and flew hundreds of combat type missions in Southeast Asia and Korea.

There was another retired officer who did not believe French's story. And that was Army Col. John Alexander.

Alexander said that during that time all they had was a laser system and the range on it was very limited. He said that in the 1980s that they were working on the pulse-power weapons but never before then.

Except for the original newspaper headline telling that the military had apprehended a UFO just out of Roswell. The USAF then closed the books that were the end of Roswell. They claimed from then on that real identity of this object was just a surveillance balloon called "Mogul."

There remained eyewitnesses-inclusive of military folks-that were telling about working the accident and their part in the cover-up of that time in Roswell. Researchers insisted that in fact, there had been an alien ship that did crash in Roswell.

French says the second crash was close to where the other one happened. It was believed that they were in that area to try and recover survivors and parts if there were any from the first crash - The UFO survivors.

French said he had seen pictures of pieces of the UFO. It had like inscriptions written on it, and they looked almost Arabic. It seemed like a part number. The pictures were just in a folder that I had thumbed through and looked.

Ex-CIA agent Chase Brandon claimed that he had found a box at the CIA headquarters in the 90s and it was labeled "Roswell."

He said he looked inside at the contents and pictures and it confirmed his thoughts about the matter that the object that had crashed at Roswell, "was not from this planet."

So, here we have French, that seems entirely credible, and he had served 27 years in the military and was an investigator for the Air Force on UFO sightings, known as Project Blue Book.

French said he was supposed to investigate and no matter what he found he was supposed to make up something, anything, but do not tell them it was a UFO.

French said, so, if someone said they saw a UFO, he along with another agent would think up a convincing explanation for the weird aberration that they had seen.

Civilians were where most of the reports came from. We would give our investigation results and debunk it by telling them it was swamp fog or what they saw had been hanging on wires. The stories went through so many channels but found their way up the ladder to the President.

But this adds to the confusion. Why was French ordered to lie about UFO reports? It did not make any sense.

French said they never gave him an explanation. But his idea on the subject was that if they ever accepted that there were aliens coming here to Earth from outside our universe or wherever it was, it could destroy religions, along with the pure fact that our military was helpless against the aliens.

And, we wouldn't want that, would we? That would not be good for the reputation of the military. French went on to say that you are talking about the effect on the military, religious reasons, and national defense.

So, it comes down to what and who you believe?

A 30-year veteran, Antonio Huneeus, a veteran who investigated UFO sightings recently spent some time with French and is working to uncover as many facts as he can about the UFOs that he supposedly said he knew about this cover up.

Huneeus said that when they started searching all they could find out about French was that he had been a combat pilot, but it showed nothing about UFOs.

Huneeus continued by saying that his reservations about the whole thing were some of the claims that French had made, and his age, his memory is probably not what it should be. It is for sure that he is very knowledgeable about UFOs, or he could have even heard about some stories or have talked to some people.

It makes it hard to separate out what he saw and what he lived and what he has read and what he has heard.

Then there is former NASA astronaut, Edgar Mitchell that came forward. He says this is all true and real. He was there when this all went down. He was on his way to college and had just graduated from high school.

One day it was in the newspaper, "Roswell Daily Record" about a UFO that had crashed. Next day it was denied. Air Force reported it was a weather balloon.

Many years after Mitchell had been to the moon; he went out to Roswell and gave lectures. He talked to the people and met a lot of them that he had known as a kid.

He said a lot of them told him their stories of the Roswell incident. The town's undertaker's son provided coffins for the alien bodies, and the sheriff's son kept the traffic away from the crash site.

Speaking of the aliens, Mitchell says, they sure are not human. They look like the little greys. He went on to add that we have no idea what beings are out in the Universe because our planet is much likened to a grain of sand on a beach when it comes to the whole universe.

Mitchell was the sixth man to take that walk out on the moon. He was on the Apollo 14 in 1971.

Mitchell had a family friend who happened to be a major in the USAF. When Mitchell heard the stories from all these people when he had gotten back from the moon, he went to the Pentagon and told his friend about the stories. He asked his friend what his opinion was about it.

The admiral said he did not know anything about it, but he would check into it.

The admiral went out to Roswell, checked out some leads, came back and got in touch with Mitchell and told him that everything that he had heard was true.

Mitchell also said that they found both live and dead aliens on the UFO. The USAF covered up the whole thing because they were not sure if these 'visits' were friendly or hostile and did not want Russia to know anything about it.

Mitchell knew of many UFO flights that came to Earth while an astronaut at NASA and every one of them were covered up.

When Hellyer was being interviewed by Tucker Carlson, and Tucker asked him if UFOs were real. Hellyer told him, "for the last two to three years I have been looking at the evidence and assessing it much as a judge would, trying to determine who was telling the truth and who wasn't, and I finally concluded, especially after reading a book called The Day After Roswell written by Col. Philip Corso, that UFOs are in fact as real as the planes flying overhead, and there has been a monumental cover-up for more than half-century.

"This is after looking at a lot of evidence in trying to discern who was telling the truth and who wasn't, and I have concluded unequivocally that the people who claim that they have either seen UFOs or seen classified documents bout UFOs, or have seen wreckage from the crash at Roswell on or about July 4, 1947, are the ones who are really telling the truth. I am consequently, basing my considerations on that."

Tucker, in turn, asked him if it made any sense then if they were buzzing our planet, wouldn't we want to defend ourselves from then if they should turn hostile.

Hellyer replied, "Well, I think the critical question is if they are hostile? Right after the crash first occurred in Roswell, General Twining declared that there were enemy aliens. There is no evidence that I have seen that would convince me that they are in fact enemies.

What would I like to know is whether that classification of enemy aliens still exists and if it does exist, what is the evidence that the U.S. government have that it bases its conclusion on?

Ex-Air Force air-man Karl Wolf says he was a precision electronics photographic repairman and had top secret clearance for the crypto area in the USAF. He was stationed at Langley in the mid-50s. He had been loaned to the project for NASA on the lunar orbiter.

He had to go into the lab where the equipment was not working, and about thirty minutes after working, one of the techs said to him in a nervous way that they had discovered a 'base' on the moon on the back side of it. He then proceeded to lay down the pictures in front of me.

No doubt these pictures were of buildings, buildings shaped like mushrooms, buildings shaped into spheres and there were towers, and at that point, he got worried because he knew he was looking at some top-secret stuff and he had breached security. He was so scared at the moment that he did not say anything more.

Donna Hare was working for a NASA supplier and said she learned real quickly about all the cover-ups. She worked for Philco-Ford Aerospace during the time of 1967-1981.

She was a design engineer/illustrator-draftsman. She worked on the landing slides, launches slides, and even projected lunar maps for NASA.

She said they were just contractors but the majority of her time she was working in Building B. She had the chance to do extra work through downtime, between missions. She happened to walk into the photo lab, which was NASA lab across the hall.

She had the secret clearance and was free to go in there. One of the techs called her attention to a picture that had a dot on it. She asked him if that was a dot on the emulsion?

He grinned and had his hands crossed. He said round dots on the emulsion would not leave shadows on the ground below.

This specific picture was of the Earth. There were shadows of an air- craft, but she did not know what it was, she just knew it was secret, one that was to be kept secret.

She asked him what they usually do with information like this, and he said he always airbrushed them out before they were showed to the public.

Edgar Mitchell told WPTV that he didn't know where, how many, or how they are doing it, but they have been out there observing us for some time. We see their aircraft all the time. I totally believe what I am saying, and I can cite the evidence as I know it.

When asked about how many civilizations he thinks are out in the universe Mitchell says, "Billions."

Mitchell is one of twelve who have walked on the moon. He will tell you he has never seen a little alien, but he does believe the people who say they have.

In 1958, Donald Keyhole, who was a retired Marine and a UFO specialist, was going to appear on TV. He was going to talk about UFOs, and the Air Force was going to "pre-sensor" the show.

As the show was going on, and he tried to tell original statements that had not been in the "pre-censored" script, the TV station would cut out his sound. They told him later he was about to violate security standards.

John Callahan, a former Division Chief of the Accident and Investigations Branch of the Federal Aviation Authority in Washington told that in 1986 that after a Japanese 747 plane had encountered a giant UFO over Alaska, it had been recorded by the radar in the air and on the ground.

The FAA started with their investigation, Callahan held a briefing for the President's Group and other intelligence offices.

Right after one of the briefings, one of the CIA agents that were there told Callahan, "They were never there, this never happened." He gave the rationale that this would cause wide spread panic for the public.

So, WHY is the government working so hard with the cover-up UFO sightings? What, are they really afraid of? Is it really mass panic? That just does not smell right. I can see where it would have been in 1947, but not in today's time.

Gee whiz, we have an orbiting space station. They probably have parties with the aliens and know a lot of the little guys by their first name.

I am about to tell you about a young man who goes by the name of 'Jordan.' Jordan claims he was more or less genetically engineered by the 'Tall Greys' so he was an abductee? He was born in 1962. Now, supposedly, his mother was also abducted and the 'Tall Greys' infused her eggs with some kind of genetic coding to make him, 'Jordan.'

Jordan feels convinced that when he was six years old he was abducted by an 'alien' or 'non-human' sentiment beings. Jordan says that those that abducted him looked like the 'Grey 'Breeders' but he could not remember seeing any 'Workers' at the time.

Jordan does not feel that the Department of the Navy has anything really to do with the United States Navy.

The Greys seem to be divided into some sort of Quasi-sentient WORKERS that are asexual and on the average about four feet tall. There are some who are the dominant BREEDERS and they have very large eyes and they are about six feet tall. Both types of the Greys have on each hand, four fingers.

The government is not fair to the citizens of the United States. We can handle some grown up talk about space and some grey or white or reptilian people. For Pete's sake.

What Really Goes On At Area 51

To say gaining access to Area 51 is limited, well, that is an understatement at best. The base and all its activities are considered highly classified. The location alone helps keep its activities "under the radar," as does being close to the Nevada Test site, where nuclear devices have and are tested.

If you happen to gain access, you will need top security clearance, an invitation from highest ranks of military or intelligence.

The government has gone to a lot of trouble making it hard to see what is going on in Area 51.

Everyone working in Area 51, whether they are civilian or military, must sign an oath agreeing that no matter what they see or hear, has to be kept secret. The buildings have no windows. Employees are not allowed to see what other employees are doing or what they are working on.

I am sorry, this may be top secret, but it all sounds like child's play to an extreme. Signing an "agreement" you will keep your mouth shut? Or what? Will they kill you? What will happen if you don't keep your mouth shut?

After all, it is out in the middle of nowhere, in Nevada's barren desert, a dusty road, unmarked that goes right up to the gate leading into Area 51. You would think it would be under more closely guarded access. But, don't worry, "they" are watching.

Beyond that gate, there are cameras focused to see every angle everywhere. Sitting on a distant hilltop will be a white truck with tinted windows watching everything going on below.

The locals say that inside the base that the know ever rabbit and turtle that crosses the barrier under the fence. Some even claim that there are sensors embedded in the soil.

What really happens inside Area 51 has led to years of mystery and speculation. There remain the alien conspiracies and the fact that aliens are housed there. One theory exists that from the 1947 Roswell crash was really a Soviet crash that had been flown there by mutated midgets and it is still inside Area 51.

And, there are those that believe man did not land on the moon, but that the U.S. government filmed the moon landing inside one of the hangars on the base.

For all the legends and myths, one thing is for sure; Area 51 is still very active and very real.

When WWII was over, the Soviet Union lowered its Iron Curtain not only around themselves but the rest of the Eastern bloc, and it created a near blackout for intelligence for the rest of our world.

The Soviets backed North Korea when they invaded South Korea in 1950. It was very clear at this point that the Kremlin would be aggressive in expanding its influence. America was worried about the USSR's intentions, technology and their ability to launch a surprise attack and coming only ten years from the Japanese attacking Pearl Harbor.

In the early 1950's, the U.S. Air Force and Navy sent low-flying aircraft on inspection missions over the USSR, at the risk of being shot down. November 1954, President Eisenhower gave approval for the secret development of high-altitude aircraft; the U-2 program. They decided to use Area 51 for the testing and training ground.

In 1980, the U.S. government said it was time to clean up Area 51 and remove the irradiated soil that was around Groom Lake. Photos taken by satellite confirm that massive amounts of dirt were removed from that area by the crews sent in to clear it out.

In the surrounding cities, there were increased rates of cancer, and many sued the government (all with different levels of success), through claims that the tests carried out there caused them to be sick.

There was a hazard involving disposal of vehicles and classified technology. Sometime in the 1980s, crews dug open, large pits and dropped toxic materials down into them.

They then burned the dumped toxins using jet fuel. Many suffered from the exposure to the fumes and the chemicals. The workers asked for safety equipment such as breathing equipment/respirators but were refused due to budget.

The employees asked if they could bring their own equipment and they were told no, it was a security risk. Several became very ill from the exposure, two died. A lawsuit was filed. It was dismissed because it would breach national security.

You wonder if living close to a place like Area 51 would make you a little weird. If you visit the little town of Rachel, Nevada your wondering might turn to certainty.

Rachel's population is 100 people. They
have a very strong sense of independence
and are a little eccentric.

According to Glenn Campbell, who used to
live in Rachel, the town's history began
March 22, 1978, at precisely 5:45 p.m. I
doubt you will find many towns can narrow
their town's origins down to that precise
time.

Campbell tells that on that day, was the first-
time power companies supplied the Valley
of Sand Springs with electricity. Before then,
only a few farmers and a mining company
lived here.

In the 1970's, people with a pioneering spirit
started coming to the area. They came

because they just wanted to live a life quiet and free of any interference. Among those people was the Jones family. They were immediately famous when they had their first child, little Rachel, so everyone decided to name the town after Rachel.

The Joneses didn't live there much longer, and sadly, a few years went by, and Rachel died from a respiratory problem.

The town of Rachel has a gas station (well, it's closed right now and the next closest gas station is 60 miles away), a bar called the Little A'Le'Inn (which is a group of mobile homes organized into a kind of motel) and then there is the Rachel Senior Center Thrift Store.

The Thrift Store is a mystery itself. Clothes come from Tonopah Thrift Shop that is 100 miles away. Rachel's little store then sends unsold clothing to the thrift stores out in Las Vegas. Then the stores in Las Vegas send unsold clothes to the Tonopah Thrift Shop. Everybody thinks this cycle will keep on going until one of the stores closes.

Joe and Pat Travis manage the Little A'Le'Inn and have a business selling videos and T-shirts about aliens and government conspiracies.

Most of the folks who live in Rachel will say they don't believe there are any UFOs. They all think it is just military aircraft, flares, and UAVs.

People who live in Rachel just take everything in stride. When a sonic boom goes off in the middle of the night or there is a bright light show, so what, it has all become the norm.

Almost everyone has had to replace a window or two that got cracked by a sonic boom or picked up a piece of airplane that landed outside of Area 51 after a wreck.

It is believed now that Area 51 is no longer the perfect hiding place for alien study. It is felt that the BIG top secret military base in Dulce, New Mexico is the new location. It is the most restricted location in the US. It is #3 on the list of 20 most restricted on earth.

Recently, John Podesta, former chief of staffer for President Bill Clinton, advisor to President Bill Clinton and Campaign Manager for Hillary Clinton has added his name to a growing list of figures of the government figures that are making little comments and hinting that they know things about aliens that no one else knows.

For instance, in a CNN interview, Podesta opened his mouth and stuck his foot in it, shoe and all when he said that the time had come for the government to "release any evidence it has/had about the existence of alien forms of life in outer space."

He fell a little short of confirming that aliens do exist and that the government has evidence of such – but all it took was his carefully placed comments that strongly suggested that he was in on knowing what was going on.

When he was pushed into a corner and asked point blank if he had seen himself proof of alien life. Podesta was carefully evasive in his response when he said, that it is for the public to judge once they have seen all the evidence that the government holds.

The reporter conducting the interview sensed there was more, so he asked Podesta if he believed in aliens. The reporter was told that there are plenty of planets out there. The people of American can handle the truth.

Is Podesta credible? His credibility comes into question when you look back at some of the things he was involved with during the Clinton campaign in 2016.

In 2005, Canada's former Defense Minister, Paul Hellyer, openly accused the major world governments of deliberately holding back important information that would prove the existence of extraterrestrial beings.

When Hellyer recently spoke at the University of Calgary, he stated that the Aliens had been coming to earth for thousands of years now. He insists that the little guys have been part of developing the LED lights, his microchip, and the Kevlar vest.

There is believed to be 'now' a base even more top secret than Area 51. It is at Dulce, New Mexico.

In 1979, Paul Bennewitz, an American business man was convinced he was getting communications from aliens (yes, I said aliens) outside Albuquerque, New Mexico in a town called Dulce.

The area where he finally figured the signals were coming from was the Dulce base; a joint alien-government biogenetic lab that carries out experiments on animals and humans.

The upper level is supposedly run by the U.S. government. The lower level is reported to be run by the aliens.

Phil Schneider, a man who helped build an entrance to this top-secret area, was found in his apartment dead, by a piano wire wrapped around his neck.

Richard Sauder, Ph.D., shared in his book 'Hidden in Plain Sight' that should be told to this audience reading this book.

After Sauder had given a talk about one of his books, he was approached by a gentleman who in his prior days had been with the United States Navy, actually a uniformed member. They chatted for a bit and then he mentioned about some time on China Lake he had spent. Sauder's ears immediately perked up!

Sauder asked him if there was an underground military facility there. He said there sure was, and it was very deep and very large. Sauder then asked if he had ever been inside of it, and he affirmed that he had but not down to the deepest levels.

Sauder, not letting up asked how deep it went down into the ocean and the man replied, 'one mile.' Sauder came back with another question then. What is housed in this location? To which the man replied, "Weapons. Weapons more powerful than nuclear weapons."

Now, there are documents available if you look for them that show deep underground centers that were going to be built far below regions such as at China Lake, California and in Washington D.C. during the time of the Cold War.

It is a well-known fact that the Soviet Union and the United States developed a huge infrastructure to keep a complex of defensive and offensive weapons during the Cold War.

The infrastructure would include facilities that tested stored, manufactured and developed weapons. There was along with this a host of command and communications centers.

November 7th, 1963 the first TOP SECRET memo about the subject came out from the Secretary of Defense office. A second memo followed on that same day in regard to a proposal to build a Deep Underground

National Command Center which would be approximately 3,500 feet below Washington. This memo further explained that there would be elevator shafts under the White House and the State Department which would drop 3,500 feet, at very high speed, and also transport in a horizontal tunnel to the main facility.

Just think about it, this was in the 1960's. Can you imagine with all the new technology what it must be like today?

Close

So, in reality, this has been going on for years. Even I can remember hearing talk of "Roswell." You do not ever forget something like that. I honestly do not think that anyone of this generation would be scared if they met an ET.

I have a work acquaintance who lives in Roswell and he is certain that there were aliens in that spaceship that day and he is sure some of them did not live. He also knew the funeral home director who had to special order small hermetically sealed caskets for Area 51 right after the crash.

However, he does not think that there is any surviving in Area 51 today. He feels if they are living, they have been moved to another location.

With the way people choose to dress, and some wear their hair and the body art they exhibit in order to show their individuality and self-expression of which I have no problem with, let me add. Seeing an ET would look "normal" anymore.

Do I think there are aliens or there were aliens that day in Roswell? I do. I can say, that I have no doubt that they found aliens in all that wreckage. Were there survivors? I have a good feeling there were.

Whether they are still alive I must wonder. I am not sure our way of life agrees with their survival. I am not sure what their longevity is either.

Do I think there is life on other planets? Absolutely! Of that I am almost certain. Why wouldn't there be? God did not have to stop here, at Earth central with his creations.

We may never know the truth, the whole truth and nothing but the truth about Area 51, but I, for one, am fine with what I do know.

At one point I was curious, but not anymore. It's just not as important as it used to be. Area 51 I am afraid has moved on to brighter and greener or maybe wetter pastures.

Do I think we will ever encounter aliens in our lifetime? Very possibly, I sure hope so. I have a lot of questions I would like to ask.

Don't you?

Printed in Great
Britain
by Amazon